Bible Stories for Young People

Volume I

C O N S T A N C E   M O R R O W

ISBN 978-1-63844-289-9 (paperback)
ISBN 978-1-63844-290-5 (digital)

Christian Faith Publishing
832 Park Avenue
Meadville, PA 16335
www.christianfaithpublishing.com

Printed in the United States of America

Contents

Preface.. 1

Acknowledgment 3

Who Made the World? 7

The Woman and Man Who Exchanged their Home and All
    They Had for Forbidden Fruit 11

The Voyage of the Big Boat 17

The Boy Who Lost His Home by Mocking............................ 23

The Young Man Who an Angel Saved 29

The Young Man Who Traded His Inheritance for a Dish of
    Pottage 33

The Beautiful Coat.. 37

The Boy Captive Who Became Prime Minister 44

A Baby's Cry That Won His Way to a Palace 50

A Fit of Anger That Cost a Good Man His Life 55

How Snake Bites Were Healed 59

A Band That Captured a City by Marching Around It
    Thirteen Times... 61

The Woman Who Used a Red Cord to Save Her Life............. 66

The Man Who Could Not Keep His Hands from Beautiful
    Things... 71

Preface

These are selected Bible stories that children and youth who are learning the Bible for the first time or on an ongoing basis should know.

Great effort has been put forth to write this study or reference book exactly based upon biblical facts using a King James Version.

This book is written for those of the believing community who want to provide a resource for children and young people who have begun their spiritual walk in life or the nonbelieving community who is simply curious as to why we believe as we do in the Lord Jesus Christ. Because one is directed to read scriptures throughout, this book may be used on an ongoing basis as a reference book, a gift, or a way to begin the lifelong journey your child takes in learning and understanding the Bible.

Children and youth will enjoy this book of Bible stories, will learn new words and phrases, will be able to contemplate a moral or character lesson, and may use this in all types of classes or presentation events such as youth activities in training and biblical exercises, oratorical competitions, or in any situation wherein Bible instruction is taking place.

These are not just stories about people but also stories about what some may define as miracles, extraordinary events that reveal divine intervention in a human condition or affair. Some may say these are myths, fairy tales, or tall tales; but those of us who believe in the birth, crucifixion, death, and resurrection of Jesus Christ know in our heart that this is the true and living Word of God.

There are four volumes of fourteen stories: Volume 1 begins with Genesis 1 and ends with Joshua 7. Volume 2 begins with Judges 6 and ends with 2 Samuel 18. Volume 3 begins with 1 Kings 7 and ends with Daniel 6. Volume 4 begins with three fish stories: Jonah 1, 2; Luke 5; and John 21. The volume ends with Acts 28.

The writing is guided by the words of 2 Timothy 3:14–17, which says,

> But continue thou in the things which thou hast learned and hast been assured of, knowing of whom thou hast learned And that from a child thou hast known the holy scriptures, which are able to make thee wise unto salvation through faith which is in Christ Jesus. All scripture [is] given by inspiration of God, and [is] profitable for doctrine, for reproof, for correction, for instruction in righteousness: That the man of God may be perfect, thoroughly furnished unto all good works.

Acknowledgment

I thank God for the life and leadership of our beloved Pastor, Dr. W. N. Daniel of Antioch Missionary Baptist Church (1957–1999). He served God by shepherding the congregation, teaching, and pastoring a multitude of believing Christians. Pastor Daniel laid a foundation of love and nourishing fellowship of believers.

I want to acknowledge the general Sunday school superintendent, Reverend Robert Wells, who I met and supervised all of us at our church, Antioch Missionary Baptist Church, in Chicago.

Reverend Wells, deceased, always wanted the people of the Sunday School to learn, understand, and know the Bible, so he made a special effort to impart knowledge from himself to the various department superintendents and to the students. He provided a variety of outlines, syllabi, and other materials for this purpose.

It is from one of his outlines dated January 1, 1984, of which I've maintained, and I have used to identify the many important Bible stories for children.

To my loving and supportive husband, Albert, who gave me "space, support, and delicious food" to relax in my writing so that I could do my best, thank God!

Jewish nation (KJV), the nation called Israel, later called Jews. This nation of people whose purpose was to know and tell others about God.

"God chose the ancient Israelites because He had *promised Abraham* that his descendants would become a great nation and occupy the land of Canaan" (Genesis 12:3, 7; 17:4, 7–8; 22:17). God *blessed Abraham* and his descendants because of Abraham's faith, a living faith that resulted in diligent obedience to God's instructions and law (Genesis 26:3–5). This promise was repeated to Abraham's son Isaac and to Abraham's grandson Jacob (Genesis 17:21; 26:24; 28:1–4, 13).

God's purpose in choosing Israel was for them to be a model nation to other nations and that through them "all the families of the earth" would be blessed (Genesis 12:3). He wanted Israel to be "a kingdom of priests and a holy nation" (Exodus 19:6). Other nations would see that when the Israelites obeyed God, they were blessed (v. 5); and when they disobeyed God, they would be punished (Deuteronomy 28).

"God chose the nation of Israel to be the people through whom Jesus Christ would be born—the Savior from sin and death (John 3:16). God first promised the Messiah after Adam and Eve's fall into sin (Genesis ch. 3). God later confirmed that the Messiah would come from the line of Abraham, Isaac, and Jacob (Genesis 12:1–3). Jesus Christ is the ultimate reason why God chose Israel to be His special people. God did not need to have a chosen people, but He decided to do it that way. Jesus had to come from some nation of people, and God chose Israel."

"However, God's reason for choosing the nation of Israel was not solely for the purpose of producing the Messiah. God's desire for Israel was that they would go and teach others about Him. Israel was to be a nation of priests, prophets, and missionaries to the world. God's intent was for Israel to be a distinct people, a nation who pointed others toward God and His promised provision of a Redeemer, Messiah, and Savior. For the most part, Israel failed in this task. However, God's ultimate purpose for Israel—that of bringing the Messiah into the world—was fulfilled perfectly in the Person of Jesus Christ." (This was a compilation and summary of statements and quotes from material gathered online from the question, "Why did God choose Israel to be His chosen people?")

Muslim nation (KJV), descendants of Abraham and Hagar.

Gentiles (KJV), all other peoples of the world, often translated as "heathen" in the Bible.

Abraham, descendant of Shem whose father was Noah, chosen by God to start a new nation that would belong to God in a special way and would be His witness among all the other nations that had turned their backs on Him.

Type (v. 9), "a type can be an object, a person, a custom, or a happening to give us something to understand. It is real itself, but it pictures something far greater than itself; A model, representation" (*Merriam-Webster*).

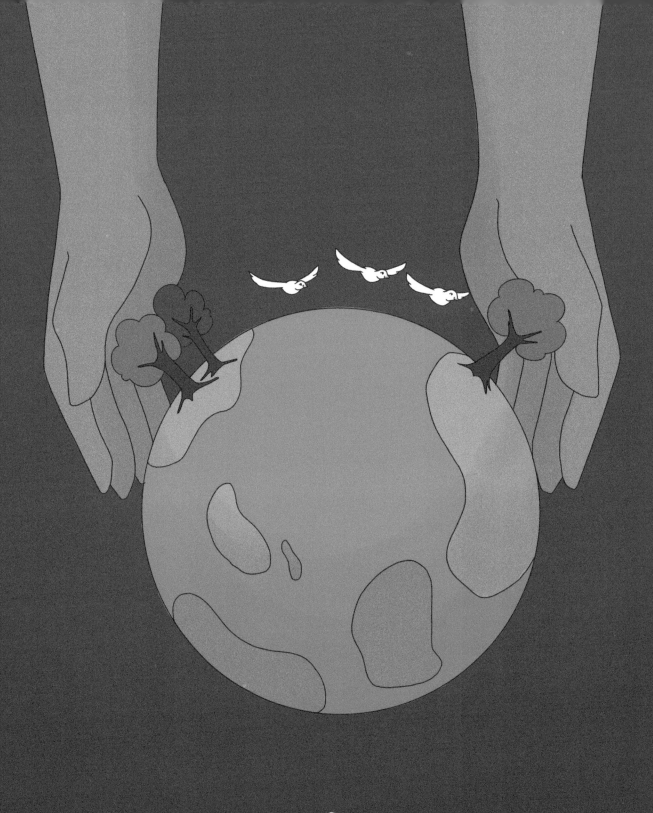

Who Made the World?

Genesis 1:1-25

Words/phrases you should know before you read:

without form and void (1:2 ESV). This means "not finished in its shape and as yet uninhabited by creature."

firmament (1:6 ESV). God made the firmament and divided the waters above and below it and calls this "heaven." It is the first heaven; the atmosphere where the birds fly and clouds form. The second heaven is where the stars and planets make up the universe.

Please note that the Apostle Paul in 2 Corinthians 12:2 spoke of the third heaven as God's dwelling place that surpasses our universe (see also 1 Kings 8:27).

after his kind (1:11 KJV). A limit was put upon every created thing so that it could never become or produce any other kind of creature. Examples: From only two chickens, many varieties of chickens can be produced, but never anything else than chickens. Apple seeds will never grow into peach trees, nor a monkey into a man.

dominion (1:26 KJV). This defined man's unique relation to creation. Man was God's representative in ruling over the creation. The command to rule separated him from the rest of living creation and defined his relationship as above the rest of creation (see reference Psalm 8:6–8).

Have you ever looked around, looked up in the sky, had an opportunity to see something beautiful and magnificent and asked yourself, Who created this? How did all this come to be? How is life created?

In the first book of the Old Testament, in the book of Genesis, we read God inspired writers to write about Him and how He created the world and life in it.

Read each section of verses of Genesis identified:

Read verses 3–5 of chapter 1. On the First Day, light and darkness, day and night, were created.

In verses 6–8, the Second Day, the firmament was formed in a division of waters above and below.

On the Third Day, the earth is named as dry land; the gathering together of the waters is called the seas; and plant life was formed on earth in verses 9–13.

The sun and moon were created on the Fourth Day to divide day and night, to identify seasons, days, and years. Stars were also formed in verses 14–19.

On the Fifth Day in verses 20–23, God created animal life in the heaven, on the earth, and in the seas.

God created beasts and creeping things after his kind. Also on this Sixth Day, God created man in His own image in verses 24–27.

The Woman and Man Who Exchanged their Home and All They Had for Forbidden Fruit

Genesis 2:8–3:15, 24

KNOWING RIGHT FROM WRONG

Words/Phrases you should know before you read:

subtil (3:1), "changed to subtile, the subtle, meaning not direct, clever, crafty; delicately suggestive." (*Merriam-Webster*)

sin (KJV), the voluntary departure of a moral agent from a known rule of rectitude or duty, prescribed by God; any voluntary transgression of the divine law, or violation of a divine command; a wicked act; iniquity. Sin is either a positive act in which a known divine law is violated, or it is the voluntary neglect to obey a positive divine command, or a rule of duty clearly implied in such command. Sin comprehends not action only, but neglect of known duty, all evil thoughts purposes, words and desires, whatever is contrary to God's commands or law. (1 John 3; Matthew 15; James 4)

A struggle of good vs. evil is within each of us was bought upon us by Adam and Eve in the Garden of Eden. Many, many years ago, at the beginning of man, God made provisions for Adam so that he would not want or need anything. At verse 8 of chapter 2, it says, "And the Lord God planted a garden eastward in Eden; and there he put the man who he had formed." God gave man the first of eight covenants: the Edenic covenant. It was a covenant between God and man. Read Genesis 2:16. There was one thing, though, that God instructed. He said to Adam at Genesis 2:17, "But of the tree of knowledge of good and evil, thou shalt not eat of it; for in the day that thou eatest thereof thou shalt surely die."

As time went on during the creation and the naming of every living creature, in His wisdom, God, said, "It is not good that the man should be alone; I will make him an help meet for him" (v. 18).

Adam continued to name every living creature. God, at this time, decided to give Adam a mate. Let's read Genesis 2:21–25 to find out what God did.

From the introduction, we know and have learned that evil was also present at the beginning of creation. We see the presence of evil at Genesis 3:1, when this presence, in the form of a serpent, begins to tempt the woman, Eve. Now remember God's instruction to Adam: "But of the tree of knowledge of good and evil, thou shalt not eat of it." Adam had clear instructions. (Think about how many instructions you receive from your parents, teachers, or others who may oversee your care.) The serpent in Genesis is described as "more subtil" than any beast of the field which the Lord God had made." The serpent asks Eve, "Yea, hath God said, Ye shall not eat of every tree of the garden?" Read how Eve responds at Genesis 3:2, 3.

Eve was faced with a decision, and she made the wrong choice. (Remember when you were asked earlier to think about instructions you receive from your parents and others. How often do you have to make a decision or choice that may be a good one or a bad one?)

Reading on your own: Genesis 3:4–7.

Let's find out the consequences or results of Adam's and Eve's bad decision.

Read Genesis 3:6, 7. An act of disobedience has occurred. This act, taking the fruit of the tree of knowledge of good and evil, is known as the Fall of Man.

Why did Eve do it? Eve saw that it was good for food, pleasant to look at, and may make her wise (taste, touch, thought). Isn't this the same thing that happens to us today? We see something that we may want to do, eat, touch, see, or think it will satisfy us in some way, so "we go for it," even though we may have been told that it is not good for us, a danger to us or something we should not have.

Even though Eve's actions resulted in the Fall of Man, which had allowed Satan, the presence of evil, to have influence within human affairs in the world as we know it, God did not leave us without hope and promise.

He promised us salvation in Genesis 3:15 when he said, "And I will put enmity between thee and the woman, and between thy seed and her seed; it shall bruise thy head, and thou shalt bruise his heel." In this verse, theologians say that a Saviour is promised. God let us know that a child would be born of a woman. and this child, God's Son, would destroy Satan. Satan would bruise the heel of the woman's son, meaning that "sin would result in the physical death of the body of God's Son, but not His mind or soul. The Son will eventually destroy Satan and we have the promise of this destruction in the Son's death and resurrection."

Adam's failure to follow God's instructions and the disobedience of Adam and Eve resulted in the Fall of Mankind and the second covenant given by God called the Adamic covenant. The conditions under which fallen man must live are the following:

1. The serpent, Satan's tool, is cursed (v. 14).
2. A Savior is promised (v. 15).
3. The state of the woman is changed (v. 16).
4. Life will be full of sorrow (v. 17).
5. Man will toil, work, on the earth (vv. 18, 19).
6. Life will end in death (v. 19).

What does this mean for us now today? It means that the presence of evil will be with us every day of our lives until our death. It means that we have a sure weapon to defeat any presence of evil: the Holy

Spirit and prayer to God in the name of His Son, Jesus Christ. In every choice, in every decision, we must rely on prayer to help us in each choice, each decision. It does not matter how little importance we place upon that decision; we must always go to God in prayer.

We can even become extremely strong and powerful. How, you ask? When we study God's Word (2 Timothy 2:15), when we always pray (Psalm 55:17; 1 Thessalonians 5:17), the strength of the Holy Spirit becomes a matchless power. The Holy Spirit will become so strong within us that we can detect and discern the presence of evil instantly, and guess what?

We have another even mightier weapon against the presence of evil. It is the wonderful, awesome, powerful name of Jesus! We don't even have to say His name. We can think His name, and He will be with us immediately. Isn't this exciting! It is *thrilling*; it gives us the ultimate joy!

I feel so happy inside, don't you? We know that each of us, no matter the color of our skin, no matter whether we have a little or a lot—we are precious in God's sight.

It is important we read God's Word, study His Word, and pray continuously. In this way, even though our lives will never be without hardships, we will be able to overcome anything that arises because of God's promises to us.

16

The Voyage of the Big Boat

Genesis 6:14–22; 7:1–24

Words/phrases you should know before you read:

ark (6:14 ESV), a hollow chest, a box designed to float on water.
(KJV) a type of the Lord Jesus Christ. It pictures for us the only way in which people can be saved from the awful judgment that God will surely bring on sin. Only those who were in the ark were saved then, and only those who are "in" the Lord Jesus Christ by having put their trust in Him will be saved when God again destroys sinners out of the earth.

gopher wood (6:14 ESV), probably wood of cedar or cypress trees.

cubit (6:15, Presbyterian reference), eighteen inches in length; equivalent to half pace, two spans, translated as cubit/yards.

have I seen righteous (7:1 KJV), Noah was not sinless, and men probably saw many faults in him. But because he had put his trust in God to save him, God, looking ahead almost 2,500 years, counted all his sin as on His Son, the Lord Jesus Christ, and all His righteousness in His Son as on Noah.

clean beasts (7:2 KJV), animals that have parted hooves, are cloven-footed and chew the cud; all in the waters that have fin and scales. See more specific information (KJV) in Leviticus 11:47 and Deuteronomy 14:3–20.

second month (7:11 KJV), second month is Iyar or Zif, May or (Presbyterian reference) 29 days between April and May.

specifications, a description of the work to be done, measurements and materials to be used. *(Merriam-Webster)*

corruption, evil, depravity, moral decay

shut (7:16 KJV), "The Lord shut him in"; a type suggesting our safety in Christ (John 10:28–29).

forty days (7:17 KJV)—it rained for forty days (v. 12). However, the flood rose higher and higher for five months, then began to go down. The water was actually on the earth from May 17 to April 1 of the next year (see 8:13). Noah was not allowed to come out until the ground was thoroughly dry, May 27 (see 8:14–16).

prevailed (7:18), remained, stayed, persisted.

A Desire for a Fresh Start

The time was such of wickedness "in the earth" that God decided He would destroy "man, beast, the creeping thing, and the fowls of the air."

Read verses 5–7.

There was only one man in whom God "found grace," and that man was Noah. Noah had three sons: Shem, Ham, and Japheth.

What do you think God meant when He said "it repenteth Him" that He had created man and other living things upon the earth?

The reference given at Zechariah 8:14 says that when repentance is used in the Old Testament, "it is used with the meaning that a person has changed his mind from man's point of view." Malachi 3:6 and Hebrews 13:8 tell us that God does not change. He knows what man will do before he does it and "what He Himself is going to do."

God saw the corruption on earth and instructed Noah to build an ark made of gopher wood. God gave Noah the exact specifications for building the ark—the length, width, height, and depth.

Read Genesis 6:12–16.

Noah was to build the ark because God had told him that He was going to "bring a flood of waters upon the earth" to destroy all flesh.

The covenant or promise God made to Noah was that all of his family will be with him in the ark.

Think about when you've made a mistake or disobeyed your parent(s) or guardian(s). You feel sorry, you want to make-up for the mistake, you want your parent(s) or guardian(s) to forgive you; or you simply want to start over, have another chance to get it right. This is what repentance and forgiveness is all about: recognizing your mistake, your wrongdoing, and asking or desiring forgiveness. That's who God is to us, One that is always willing to forgive us of our sins, our wrongdoing. Why? Because God loves us.

Read Genesis 6:19–22.

God instructed Noah to put two of every sort of animal after its kind into the ark and to store food for himself and his family. Noah did as God commanded. "And the Lord said unto Noah, Come thou and all thy house into the ark; for thee have I seen righteous before me in this generation."

Read Genesis 7:1–24.

God gave Noah instructions to take by sevens, male and his female clean beasts, and by two, male and his female unclean beasts.

To keep seed alive upon the earth, God told Noah to take fowls by sevens, male and the female.

God told Noah that, for seven days, He will cause it to rain on earth forty days and forty nights and that every living substance will be destroyed off the face of the earth.

Noah did all that God commanded and at this time he was six hundred years old. Because of the waters of the flood, Noah, his wife, his sons, and his sons' wives went into the ark

The clean beasts, unclean beasts, and the fowls went in unto Noah two and two.

For seven days, waters of the flood were upon the earth from the fountains of the great deep. The windows of heaven were opened, and the rain fell for forty days and forty nights.

Noah; his wife; his sons, Shem, Ham, and Japheth; the wives of his sons; and all the beasts, every creeping thing, every fowl after his kind, and every bird of every sort—the Lord shut them in the ark.

The flood was upon the earth for forty days. The waters increased, and the ark was lifted up above the earth.

The waters prevailed and increased greatly upon the earth, and all the high hills were covered, fifteen cubits upward.

Every living substance—all flesh, fowl, cattle, beasts, creeping thing, and man—upon the earth died.

The waters prevailed upon the earth a hundred and fifty days, and only Noah and they that were with him were alive in the ark.

Sin had overwhelmed and suffocated every living thing that God had created. God moved to begin a fresh start in His creation.

Boys and girls, young men and young ladies, sin leads to destruction.

The Boy Who Lost His Home by Mocking

Genesis 21:9–20

Words/Phrases you should know before you read:

heir (15:4), "one who inherits or is entitled to inherit" (*Merriam-Webster*)

bowels (15:4), innermost part of body; from within the body of the person

bear (16:2), to have or birth a child

discord, "lack of agreement or harmony; dissension" (*Merriam-Webster*)

circumcision (17:10; 21:4 KJV), a cut making a mark in the flesh of every male who is a descendant of Abraham as a sign that the circumcised man believes in the covenant God made with Abraham and all Abraham's descendants.

weaned (21:8), "able to take food by means other than nursing" (*Merriam-Webster*)

cast (21:10), to put out, throw out (*Merriam-Webster*)

At the time before the Lord God brought judgement upon the evilness of Sodom and Gomorrah, in Genesis 15:4, He told Abram, "This shall not be thine heir; but he that shall come forth out of thine own bowels shall be thine heir."

In Genesis 16:2, Sarai told Abram that because she could not bear him a child, she asked him to go to her maid Hagar, an Egyptian, in order to bear a child with her. Scripture tells us in Genesis 16:3 that Sarai gave Hagar to Abram to be his wife.

What Sarai had done, giving her maid to her husband as wife, was a common custom in that country according to a code of laws called Hammurabi described in Genesis 14:1. Doing this caused a problem later. Sarai's impatience and Abram's wavering of faith caused Abram to forget that "he should not follow human reason or try by his own efforts to help God fulfill any of His promises."

God needs no help to fulfill His promises or exercise His divine will. This is one of three lessons in this story.

After Sarai gave her Egyptian bondmaid, Hagar, to her husband, Abram, this second wife given to Abram bore a son named Ishmael. For Abram's household, the birth of Ishmael became a source of discord.

Before this story began in Genesis 21:9–20, God changed Abram's name to *Abraham* (Genesis 17:5), and in Genesis 17:15, God told Abraham to no longer call his wife Sarai but *Sarah*.

Read Genesis 18:1–15. The Lord God told Abraham that he his wife Sarah will have a son (18:10–13). Sarah laughed because she (18:11) had passed the point in womanhood whereby she could conceive.

Read Genesis 21:1–20.

After the destruction of Sodom and Gomorrah, as promised, the Lord God visited Sarah so that she did conceive with Abraham (Genesis 21:1–2). Sarah bore a son whom Abraham named *Isaac*.

The Lord had instructed Abraham in Genesis 17:10–14 that he was to circumcise every male child as a pledge or seal of the covenant between Him and Abraham and his belief in the covenant. It was a sign of a pledge in the certainty of God's promises.

When Isaac was eight days old, Abraham circumcised his son as God had commanded. "And Abraham was an hundred years old when his son Isaac was born unto him" (Genesis 21:5).

Sarah said that God had made her laugh and thought to herself, "Who would have said unto Abraham, that Sarah should have given children suck? [21:6–7], for I have born him a son in his old age."

As Isaac grew and was weaned, Abraham made a feast on the same day that Isaac was weaned. "And Sarah saw the son of Hagar the Egyptian, which she had born unto Abraham, mocking" (21:9).

According to Bible historians, Ishmael was at this time approximately fourteen years old.

When Sarah saw Hagar's son mocking, she told Abraham to cast Hagar and her son, Ishmael, out because she did not want Ishmael to be an heir of Abraham along with Isaac.

Read Genesis 21:10–20.

The idea of sending Hagar and Ishmael away grieved Abraham. He did not want to do this, but God instructed him to listen to Sarah as from Isaac will come the generations of Abraham.

Mocking, making fun of someone produces pain and harm.

Because Ishmael is the seed of Abraham, God told Abraham that He will make a nation through Ishmael.

Abraham got up early in the morning, took bread and a skin of water, gave it to Hagar, and then sent Hagar and Ishmael away.

Hagar and Ishmael went away. They wandered in the wilderness of Beersheba (which means "well of the oath"), that was west of Bethel and south of Hebron. After the water was finished, Hagar put Ishmael under one of the shrubs. She walked away from him because she did not want to see her child die. She cried, and God heard the voice of Ishmael. An angel of God called to Hagar from heaven and asked her, "What aileth thee, Hagar?" The angel told Hagar not to be afraid; God had heard Ishmael's voice and knew where he was. God instructed Hagar to go to Ishmael, lift him up, and hold him in her hands. God said, "For I will make him a great nation." God opened Hagar's eyes, and she saw a well of water. She went, filled the skin with water, and gave Ishmael water to drink.

"And God was with the lad; and he grew, and dwelt in the wilderness, and became an archer."

In further study, we learn that Ishmael is the forefather of the generations of Arabs and Palestinians who continue warring with the descendants of Isaac, forefather of the Jews, to this very day.

The Young Man Who an Angel Saved

Genesis 22:1–13

Words/phrases you should know before you read:

burnt offering (22:2), something offered and burnt on an altar, as an atonement for sin; a sacrifice; called also burnt-sacrifice

clave (22:3 KJV), split

abide ye here (22:5), remain here

yonder (22:5), "at or to that place; beyond" (*Merriam-Webster*)

thicket (22:13), "dense growth of bushes or small trees" (*Merriam-Webster*)

Will you grow in faith that will help you prevail a test from God? Abraham's heir is offered to the Lord. "And it came to pass after these

29

things, that God did tempt Abraham, and said unto him, Abraham: and He said, Behold here I am."

God had tempted or tested the faith of Abraham before, but here in Genesis 21:1–13, God presents the most difficult test of Abraham's faith. Abraham was instructed by God to sacrifice his beloved son, Isaac, as a burnt offering.

God instructed Abraham to take Isaac into the land of Moriah, upon a mountain of which God would tell him, to prepare the burnt offering.

Abraham got up early in the morning, put a saddle on his donkey, and took two young men with him along with his son, Isaac. He put the wood together and went to the place where God told him. At the third day, Abraham looked up and saw the place some distance away. He then told the two men to remain from where he saw the location that God wanted him to go and that he and Isaac would go there together and worship.

Abraham took the wood for the burnt offering and laid it upon Isaac. With fire and a knife in his hand, they went toward the place.

Isaac asked his father, Abraham, "Where is the lamb for a burnt offering?" Abraham told Isaac that God will provide himself a lamb for a burnt offering, and the two continued toward the place.

After getting to the place where God wanted him to go, Abraham built an altar, laid the wood in order, bound Isaac, and put him upon the altar.

As Abraham stretched forth his hand to slay Isaac, an angel of the Lord called to Abraham out of heaven and instructed him not to slay Isaac or do anything to him. The angel said, "For now I know that thou fearest God, seeing thou has not withheld thy son, thine only son, from me."

When Abraham lifted up his eyes, he saw a ram caught in a thicket by his horns, so Abraham went, took the ram, and offered him up for a burnt offering in place of his son, Isaac.

Abraham called the name of that place *Jehovah-jireh*, which means, "The Lord will provide."

Read Genesis 22:1–13 and Hebrews 11:8–10.

God rewards faith!

"But without faith it is impossible to please him [God]; for he that cometh to God must believe that he is and that he is a rewarder of them that diligently seek him" (Hebrews 11:6).

32

The Young Man Who Traded His Inheritance for a Dish of Pottage

Genesis 25:19–34

Words/phrases you should know before you read:

barren (25:21), "unable to bare children; not productive; sterile; infertile" (*Merriam-Webster*)

conceive (25:21), "becoming pregnant; to have a baby" (*Merriam-Webster*)

womb (25:23), "uterus" (*Merriam-Webster*)

threescore (25:26 KJV), being three times twenty; sixty

cunning (25:27 KJV), skillful

attractive (25:25–27 KJV reference), physically good-looking; handsome

pottage (25:29 KJV), boiled lentils

birthright (25:31 KJV), (1) the right to a double share of the father's wealth at his death. (2) the right to be priest in the family after the father's death, for women or children were not expected to have direct contact with God. In Abraham's family, the birthright included being in the direct line of the coming Saviour.

swear (25:33), "to make a solemn statement or promise under oath" (*Merriam-Webster*)

lentil (25:34), "flat, edible seed; legume" (*Merriam-Webster*)

At forty years old, Isaac married Rebekah. Isaac pleaded with the Lord to heal his wife, who was barren, so that he could have children. The Lord responded and blessed Rebekah to conceive with two children.

Rebekah felt that the two children within her struggled, so she went to the Lord to ask why this was so. The Lord said unto her, "Two nations are in thy womb, and two manner of people shall be separated from thy bowels; and the one people shall be stronger than the other people; and the elder shall serve the younger."

When it was time for Rebekah to give birth, she bore two sons. The first child came out red all over, and Isaac and Rebekah called him Esau. The second came, and he was called Jacob.

Isaac is said to have been threescore when the two boys were born.

Esau became a very cunning hunter, and Jacob was said to be plain and spent most of his time dwelling in tents. Esau is described as more manly and attractive, but did not have faith in God's sight, while Jacob honored God, believed in God's promises.

Isaac loved Esau because he ate the venison, meat from hunted animals, but Rebekah loved Jacob.

It is never wise or good to make a difference in your or other children.

While Jacob was boiling lentils, Esau had come in from the field and felt faint. Esau asked Jacob to give him some of the red pottage or boiled lentils. Once Esau received some of the red pottage, his name was then said to be *Edom*. While Esau was in this condition, Jacob said, "Sell me this day thy birthright."

Esau replied, "Behold, I am at the point to die: and what profit shall this birthright do to me?"

Jacob said, "Swear to me this day," and he (Esau) sware unto him: and he sold his birthright unto Jacob. "Then Jacob gave Esau bread and pottage of lentils; and he did eat and drink, and rose up, and went his way: thus Esau despised his birthright meaning he disregarded it as important, scorned it."

Esau, even though he was more favored by his father, Isaac, did not understand what was entailed in his birthright that he gave over to Jacob for pottage of lentils. Having birthright was always given to the firstborn son of a family. It meant being able to receive a double share of the father's wealth at his death, to become priest and have direct contact with God—and in the case of Abraham's family, it meant being in direct line of the coming Savior.

The Beautiful Coat

Genesis 37:1–34

Words/phrases you should know before you read:

peaceably (37:4 KJV, online dictionary), without war; without tumult or commotion; without private feuds and quarrels; without disturbance; quietly; without agitation; without interruption.

sheaves (37:7), bundles of wheat grain

dominion (37:8), sovereign authority; rule or power to rule

reign (37:8), the authority or rule of a sovereign (some with supreme or independent authority)

obeisance (37:9), an outward act of homage and respect

rebuked (37:10), reproved; reprehended; punished for faults

Joseph is a type of Christ because

- he was beloved by his father;
- hated and rejected by this brothers to the point that they wanted to kill him;
- he saved his people of Egypt just as Christ came and saved all people;
- he saved his brothers (Israelites) and later made himself known to them; and
- he became a ruler, exalted by his brothers just as Christ will rule the world and will make Israel the chief nation of the world.

In Genesis 37:2, we are introduced to the generations of Jacob. Joseph's great-grandfather is Abraham, and his grandfather is Isaac. They lived in the land of Canaan where they were viewed as and called foreigners even though it was the land given to Abraham by God.

Historical record says that Abraham was expecting to be a part of the heavenly city in his vision of the land God had promised during his lifetime on earth, so he lived in a tent throughout much of his life and had taught his son Isaac to live in a tent. Isaac taught his son Jacob to do so.

Joseph, who was seventeen years old at the time, was feeding the flock of their animals with his brothers, who had different mothers but all of whom were his father's children. Joseph returned from feeding a flock of sheep to give his father, Jacob, an "evil report" about his brothers.

Jacob, who was also called Israel (in Genesis 35:10), had a special love for his son Joseph particularly because Joseph was his son during the period of his old age. To show his love for Joseph, Jacob (Israel) made him a coat of many colors.

Parents should not favor one child over the other.

Sadly, his brothers saw this, and ill-feelings grew against Joseph. Scripture says, "And when his brethren (brothers) saw that their father loved him more than all his brethren, they hated him, and could not speak peaceably unto him."

Jealousy can lead to more sin.

Joseph had a dream and told his brothers about it, and it caused his brothers to hate him even more.

> "And he said unto them, hear I pray you, this dream which I have dreamed: For, behold, we were binding sheaves in the field, and lo my sheaf arose, and also stood upright and behold, your sheaves stood round about, and made obeisance to my sheaf.
>
> And his brethren said to him, shalt though indeed reign over us? Or shalt thou indeed have dominion over us? And they hated him yet the more for his dreams, and for his words.
>
> Joseph had another dream and told his brothers that he dreamed that the sun, moon and the eleven stars will humble themselves before him and obey him.

After telling his brothers and then telling his father about his dream, his father rebuked him and said, 'Shall I and thy mother and brethren indeed come to bow down ourselves to thee on the earth?'"

Joseph's brothers envied him, but his father took note of Joseph's dreams.

A time came when Joseph's brothers went to Shechem to feed their father's animals. Jacob, whose name was also Israel, asked Joseph about his brothers being in Shechem to feed the flock and told Joseph that he would send him to his brothers.

Jacob wanted Joseph to go to Shechem to see if all was well with his brothers then return to him to give a report. Joseph was found wandering in a field when a man asked him, "What seekest thou?"

Joseph said, "I seek my brethren."

The man told Joseph that he had heard his brothers say that they were going to a city called Dothan, and Joseph did find them there. His brothers saw Joseph coming from a distance, and before he came near to them, they plotted to kill him, scoffing to one another, saying, "Here, this dreamer is coming."

His brothers talked about killing Joseph and throwing his body into a pit and how they would say than an animal had eaten him. "We shall see what will become of his dreams."

Joseph's brother Reuben heard the other brothers and said, "Let's not kill him." Reuben suggested that no blood should be shed, "but cast him into this pit that is in the wilderness, and lay no hand upon him, that he might rid him out of their hands, to deliver him to his father again."

When Joseph came to his brothers, they stripped him of his coat of many colors, took him, and cast him into an empty pit, and there was no water in the pit. As the brothers sat down to eat bread, they looked up and saw a group of Ishmeelites from Gilead with camels carrying spices, balm, and myrrh headed to Egypt.

Judah spoke to his brothers and asked, "What profit is it if we slay our brother and conceal his blood?" Judah suggested selling Joseph to the traveling Ishmeelites and that he and his brothers not kill him since he was their brother and their flesh. The brothers were pleased with that idea.

As a group of Midianite merchants passed by, the brothers lifted Joseph from the pit and sold him to the Ishmeelites for twenty pieces of silver, the price of a boy. The Ishmeelites, who were descendants of Ishmael, another son of Abraham, took Joseph to Egypt.

When Reuben returned to the pit and saw that Joseph was not there, he ripped his clothes in anguish. Reuben returned to his brothers and told them that Joseph was not in the pit. Reuben asked, "Whither shall I go?"

The brothers took Joseph's coat and dipped the coat in the blood of a goat they had killed and brought Joseph's coat of many colors to their father. They told their father that they had found a coat but didn't know if it was his son's Joseph's coat.

Their father recognized the coat and said that it is his son's coat. He thought an animal had eaten and ripped Joseph to pieces. Jacob tore his clothes, put on sackcloth, and mourned over Joseph for many days.

Let's reflect for a moment. Have you ever felt jealous of someone and searched your mind and heart as to why you have those feelings? Have your parents ever made you feel that you were not as good or capable as a brother or sister or have they ever made you feel just a little less loved than one of your brothers or sisters?

This is what happened here in this story: other young people not feeling as if they received the same amount of love or that they were as special in their parents' sight. This may be seen as a picture of how hurt, bruised feelings, insecurity, and jealousy can grow into something so deep and strong that it can lead us to do something terribly wrong and ugly. This is also a picture of how Satan can see a crack or small opening into your life and widen the opening further.

This becomes a lesson that God wants us to learn so that we today do not repeat such a mistake with our children, brothers, sisters, as a parent or to anyone.

The Boy Captive Who Became Prime Minister

Genesis 37:13–36; 39:20–23; 41:1–44

Words/Phrases you should know before you read:

devoured (37:33), eaten; swallowed; consumed

rent (37:33), torn asunder; split or burst by violence

sackcloth (37:34), cloth made of black goats' hair, coarse, rough, and thick, used for sacks, and also worn by mourners

loins (37:34), the space on each side of the vertebrae, between the lowest of the false ribs and the upper portion of the osilium or haunch bone, or the lateral portions of the lumbar region

kine (41:2), cattle

rank (41:5), placed in a line; disposed in an order or class

famine (41:30), times of scarcity, little food

grievous (41:31), distressing; calamitous; great; enormous

discreet (41:33), prudent; wise in avoiding errors or evil, and in selecting the best means to accomplish a purpose; circumspect; cautious; wary; not rash

fifth part (41:34), as to give a fifth or two fifths

vestures (41:42), a garment; dress; garments in general; clothing; covering

Genesis 37:13–36

Jacob's sons and daughters tried to comfort him, but Jacob could not be comforted. He said, "For I will go down into the grave unto my son mourning." Jacob continued to cry for Joseph.

The Midianites sold Joseph in Egypt to Potiphar, an officer of Pharaoh, of his guard.

Genesis 39:20–23

Potiphar became angry and put Joseph into prison, but the Lord God was with Joseph and had mercy upon him and made the jail keeper see Joseph favorably.

The jail keeper placed all the other prisoners under Joseph, and he oversaw the prisoners and led them to do many things that pleased the jail keeper.

Read Genesis 40 to learn why Pharaoh became angry with two of his officers, the chief butler and chief baker, and how Joseph interpreted their dreams.

Genesis 41:1–44

Pharaoh dreamed two dreams that awoke him and troubled his spirit. He wanted to know what the dreams meant, so he summoned (asked for) all the magicians and wise men of Egypt. He told them his dreams, which none of them could interpret.

Pharaoh's chief butler, who had been spared from death, remembered a Hebrew servant to the captain of the guard. The chief butler told Pharaoh that the Hebrew servant had interpreted his dream and the dream of the chief baker who Pharaoh had killed.

Pharaoh sent for Joseph, and he was brought from the dungeon, whereupon he shaved himself and changed his clothing. He came before Pharaoh, and Pharaoh told Joseph of his dream that no one could interpret. "But I have heard that it is said of thee that thou canst understand to interpret it."

And Joseph answered Pharaoh, "It is not in me. God shall give Pharaoh an answer of peace."

Pharaoh told Joseph about his dreams, and Joseph told Pharaoh that God had shown him what he was about to do. Joseph interpreted that the seven good kine and the seven good ears were seven years of plenty. The seven thin and ill-favored kine and the seven empty ears would be seven years of famine.

Joseph told Pharaoh that there would be seven years of great plenty throughout all the land of Egypt, after which there will be seven years of famine. The plenty will be forgotten, and the famine will consume the land. The famine will be very grievous. Because Pharaoh had seen the dream twice, that meant that God was going to bring it to pass soon.

Pharaoh said that he will appoint officers over the land, and they will take the fifth part of the land of Egypt in the seven years of plenty. The officers would gather all the food of those good years and store it for the seven years of famine. The idea of Pharaoh was good in his sight and in the sight of his servants.

Pharaoh asked the servants, "Can we find such a one this is, a man in whom the Spirit of God is?" Pharaoh looked to Joseph and said, "There is none so discreet and wise as you, and you shall be over and rule my house and only I in the throne will be greater than you."

And Pharaoh said unto Joseph, "See, I have set thee over all the land of Egypt." Pharaoh took off his ring from his hand and put it upon Joseph's hand and clothed him in fine linen and a gold chain around his neck.

Joseph was to ride in the second chariot after Pharaoh, and the people cried and bowed to him. Pharaoh told Joseph that no one in the land of Egypt could lift a hand or foot without permission from him.

A Baby's Cry That Won His Way to a Palace

Exodus 2:1–10

Words/Phrases you should know before you read:

goodly (2:2), being of a handsome form; beautiful

bulrushes (2:3), a word which denotes "belonging to a marsh"

daubed (2:3), smeared with soft adhesive matter

slime and pitch (2:3), of the same nature as our petroleum, but thicker, and hardens into asphalt

The story begins that there was a man of the house of Levi who took to wife a daughter of Levi. The woman conceived and bore a son, and when she saw him, she thought that "he was a goodly child."

She hid him because the new king of Egypt did not know Joseph, who had died. The new king was afraid because the Israelites were fruitful and multiplied and had many children. The king feared

that the Israelites would overtake the Egyptians, so he ordered the Hebrew midwives to kill all newborn male babies. So the mother of this goodly child hid him for three months, even though the Hebrew midwives feared God and did not do as the king commanded. When the mother could no longer hide her son, she took him and placed him in an ark of bulrushes made of slime and pitch and laid it by the river's edge.

His sister stood some distance away and witnessed what was done.

The daughter of the Pharaoh came down to wash herself along with her maidens, who walked along the river's side. When the daughter of Pharaoh saw the ark among the wild irises, she sent one of her maids to fetch it. When Pharaoh's daughter opened it, she saw the child, who cried. She had compassion on him and said, "This is one of the Hebrew children."

The baby's sister asked Pharaoh's daughter, "Shall I go and call to thee a nurse of the Hebrew women that she may nurse the child for thee?"

Pharaoh's daughter told her to go, and the girl went and got the mother of the child. The daughter of Pharaoh told the mother, whom she didn't know was the child's mother, to nurse the baby for her and that she would pay her wages to do it.

When the child grew and the mother brought him back to Pharaoh's daughter, he became her son. Because she had drawn him out of the water, she named him *Moses*.

A Thought to Understand One Aspect of Life

Men inspired by Satan can have ill-intent, ill-will in thoughts, or actions toward others, but there are times when God intervenes divinely to change a course in someone's life. Remember the characteristics of God: He is omnipotent (all powerful), omniscient (all knowing), and omnipresent (everywhere at all times). We can cry to God in our thinking, through our mind or verbalizing a prayer, and He will hear and help us! Hallelujah, praise God!

54

A Fit of Anger That Cost a Good Man His Life

Numbers 20:10–12; Deuteronomy 3:23–26

Words/Phrases you should know before you read:

smote (37:4), to strike; to throw, drive or force against, as the fist or hand, a stone or a weapon; to reach with a blow or a weapon

sanctify (37:7), exalting them to a supreme love to God; to secure from violation; to praise and celebrate him as a holy being; to acknowledge and honor his holy majesty, and to reverence his character and laws

As the Israelites traveled toward the Promised Land, they were constantly complaining because of a lack of water and food. This angered and agitated Moses.

Moses with his brother Aaron had gathered the congregation of their people the Israelites before the rock where God had commanded that they go. Moses asked the people, "Hear now, ye rebels; must we fetch you water out of this rock?"

And Moses lifted up his rod in his hand and struck the rock twice. Water came out abundantly, and the people and their animals drank.

Because Moses did not acknowledge that the water from the rock was given by God, Moses had taken honor that belonged to God. He had made the people think that the water came from him, not that he was following God's command. "And the Lord spake unto Moses and Aaron, Because ye believed me not, to sanctify me in the eyes of the children of Israel, therefore ye shall not bring this congregation into the land which I have given them."

Moses had made mistakes and had come to learn the importance of obeying God and the law he and the Israelites had been given at Sinai. Moses spoke to God and said, "O Lord God, thou has begun to shew thy servant thy greatness, and thy mighty hand: for what God is there in heaven or in earth, that can do according to thy works and according to thy might?"

God had done many things for Moses and the people of Israel.

Moses asked God to let him go over to see the good land beyond Jordan and Lebanon. The Lord was angry with Moses and would not listen to him. He told Moses not to speak with him again concerning the land that was the Promised Land to the people of Israel.

God commanded Moses to go to the top of Pisgah to look in every direction and see the land in which he shall not go. Moses was to charge and encourage Joshua, his heir, to lead the people to the Promised Land.

Because Moses had rebelled against God in the desert of Zin and wanted to exalt himself before the people, he lost his life and opportunity to go to the land God had promised the people of Israel.

Life Lesson

Everything we do, every gift or talent we have, is by the grace of God, who should receive our praise and thanks. We can quickly experience loss when we want to take credit or glory from what was originated by God.

How Snake Bites Were Healed

Numbers 21:4–9

Words/Phrases you should know before you read:

loatheth (21:5),—hate; dislike strongly

After the Lord had delivered the Canaanites in battle into the hand of Israel, they resumed their journey under the leadership of Moses. As they journeyed from the battleground in Hormah by way of the Red Sea to circle the land of Edom, the people become discouraged.

As they had done in the past, the people began murmuring, whispering complaints against God and against Moses. They asked, "Wherefore have ye brought us out of Egypt to die in the wilderness? For there is no *bread*, neither is there any water; and our soul *loatheth this light* bread (manna)."

And the Lord *sent* fiery serpents among the people, and they *bit* many people of Israel, and they died.

The people then came to Moses, pleading for him to pray to the Lord to take *the* serpents from them. They admitted that they had spoken against the Lord and against Moses. So the Lord said unto Moses, "Make thee a fiery serpent and set it upon a pole; and it came to pass, that every one that is bitten, when he *looketh* upon it, shall live."

And Moses made a serpent of brass and put it upon a pole so that if a serpent had *bitten* any man, when he *looketh* at the brass serpent, he lived.

Reflection

The serpent was a type of *sin*, and brass was a type of judgment.

When God commanded Moses to make a brass serpent, it became a *picture of sin* (rebellion of the people), being punished and (biting serpents) judged. "Whoever looked at the serpent was cured." It is a *figure* of the judgment of God against sin and of Christ, *who bore our sins*." Now anyone who trusts him—looks to him—is saved.

A Band That Captured a City by Marching Around It Thirteen Times

Joshua 6:1–20

Words/phrases you should know before you read:

straitly shut (1), "fortified, walls that provide a strong defense" (*Merriam-Webster*)

harlot (17), "those who lay under the ban of society" (*Smith's Bible Dictionary*); "a woman consecrated or devoted to prostitution" (*Easton's Bible Dictionary*)

accursed (17 KJV), doomed to destruction or misery

Jericho was a fortified city within walls, shut up where none could come in or go out because of its fear of the children of Israel.

> And the Lord said unto Joshua, "See, I have given into thine hand Jericho, and the king thereof, and the mighty men of valour."
>
> God instructed Joshua to circle the city with his armies and go around once for six days.
>
> Seven priests were to carry seven trumpets of rams' horns before the ark and on the seventh day they were to circle the city seven times blowing their trumpets.
>
> After a long blast with the ram's horn and when the people hear the sound of the trumpet all of the people were to shout a great shout. When they shout the great shout the wall of the city of Jericho shall fall down flat, and the people shall overtake everyone from Jericho before them.
>
> And Joshua the son of Nun called the priests, and said unto them, "Take up the ark of the covenant, and let seven priests bear seven trumpets of rams' horns before the ark of the Lord."

He told the people to go on, circle the city, but let those that are armed go before the ark of the Lord. The seven priests did so, blowing the trumpets, followed by the ark of the covenant of the Lord. The armed men were before the priests who blew the trumpets, and the troops in the rear followed. "And Joshua had commanded the people, saying, Ye shall not shout, nor make any noise with your voice, neither shall any word proceed out of your mouth, until the day I bid you shout; then shall ye shout."

The ark of the Lord circled the city once, and they gathered and lodged in the camp.

Joshua rose early in the morning, and the priests took up the ark of the Lord. The seven priests with seven trumpets of rams' horns continued with the ark of the Lord, the armed men in front and the rear troops following behind the ark.

On the second day, they circled the city once for six days then returned to camp.

On the seventh day, they did the same, circling the city seven times.

And it came to pass at the seventh time, when the priests blew with the trumpets, Joshua said unto the people:

> "Shout; for the Lord has given you the city.
>
> And the city shall be accursed, even it, and all that are therein, to the Lord: only Rahab the harlot shall live, she and all that are with her in the house, because she hid the messengers that we sent."
>
> You, the people, shall stay from anything forbidden unless you risk becoming accursed and bringing trouble to the camp of Israel.
>
> All treasures of Jericho belong to God, are consecrated for Him and go into the treasury of the Lord.

So the people shouted when the priests blew with the trumpets: and it came to pass, when the people heard the sound of the trumpet, and the people shouted with a great shout, that the wall fell down flat so that the people went up into the city, every man straight before him, and they took the city.

The Woman Who Used a Red Cord to Save Her Life

Joshua 2, 6:22–25

Words/Phrases you should know before you read:

harlot (2:1), Rahab was said to have been an innkeeper, however, as a Canaanite woman; historians conclude that she may have been a prostitute.

fords (2:7), A shallow place in a river or other water, where it may be passed by man or beast on foot, or by wading; a stream; a current

The Israelites had journeyed through the wilderness led by Joshua, whom Moses had given charge over them. They arrived on the eastern side of the river but still had to do battle to acquire the land of their inheritance. They were faced with a city, Jericho, with fortified walls for defense and guarded. The only way in or out was through its gates.

Joshua sent two men to spy on the land of Jericho. The two men came to the house of Rahab and stayed there.

The king of Jericho was told that these two men of Israel had come into the city at night and that they lodged with Rahab. The king sent a message to Rahab to bring the two men lodging with her to him. The king told Rahab that the men had come to search and see all the country. Rahab hid the two men of Israel and told the king that she didn't know where they had gone.

She told the king that the two men had gone away, but if he pursued them quickly, he can capture them.

Rahab hid the men on the roof of her house under stalks of flax that she had laid on the roof.

The king's men went after the two men of Israel toward the fords of Jordan. The king's men closed the gates after they had gone out of the fortress.

Rahab went upon the roof, and she spoke to the men of Israel and said that she knew that the Lord had given them the land and that all the inhabitants of Jericho and the land about were afraid of the children of Israel. She recounted how the Lord had dried up the Red Sea so that they could walk through, how the Lord delivered them out of the hands of the Egyptians, and how the armies of the Israelites had destroyed their enemies along the way.

Rahab told the men that after people had heard about these things, they knew that their God was the God in heaven and in earth.

After hiding them so that they would not be captured, Rahab wanted the men to remember the kindness she had shown to them. Rahab asked the two Hebrew men to give her a true token. She wanted her father, mother, sisters, and brothers to be spared from death.

The men answered her, saying, "Our life for yours. And it shall be, when The Lord hath given us the land, that we will deal kindly and true with thee."

Rahab then let them down by a cord through the window. Her house was upon the town wall, and she lived on the wall. She cautioned the men to get to the mountain and hide there for three days until the king's men returned. Rahab said after the pursuers returned, "Then you will be able to go on your way."

The two Hebrew men said unto her, "We will be blameless of this thine oath which thou has made us swear." They told her to tie a line of scarlet thread in that window where she had let them down. She was to bring all her family into her home. If they left her home, they would be killed, and they could not be blamed. But if any harm came to anyone inside her house, they would accept blame.

The two men also told Rahab that if she divulged anything about the oath between them, they would no longer be bound by the oath. Rahab agreed and accepted what was said, and she sent them away and tied the scarlet line in the window.

The Hebrew men stayed in the mountain for three days until they were no longer pursued. They came to Joshua and told him everything that happened and that all the inhabitants of Jericho and the surrounding lands were *afraid* of the children of Israel.

See Joshua 6:22–24.

Joshua told the two men whom he had sent as spies to go to Rahab and bring her, her family, and all she had out of Jericho. After they took Rahab and her family, they left them within the camp of Israel. They burned the entire city but put the silver, gold, vessels of brass and iron into the treasury of the house of the Lord.

After being saved by Joshua, Rahab and her family lived in Israel among the Hebrews.

Read Joshua 6:25.

The Man Who Could Not Keep His Hands from Beautiful Things

Joshua 7

Words/phrases you should know before you read:

trespass (7:1), to commit any offense or to do any act that injures or annoys another; to violate any rule of rectitude to the injury of another; In a moral sense, to transgress voluntarily any divine law or command; to violate any known rule of duty

accursed thing (7:1), doomed to destruction or misery: worthy of the curse; detestable; execrable; wicked; malignant in the extreme.

dissembled (7:11), concealed under a false appearance; disguised

The Israelites had conquered and destroyed Jericho but later suffered defeat when one man caused the whole of Israel to sin. The man Achan committed the trespass. Because of Achan's trespass, God allowed Israel to be defeated in battle with the Amorites.

Joshua tore his clothes and fell to the earth before the ark of the Lord because of the punishment that had befallen them. The Lord said to Joshua:

> Get thee up; wherefore liest thou thus upon thy face?
>
> Israel hath sinned, and they have also transgressed my covenant which I commanded them: for they have even taken of the accursed thing, and have also stolen, and dissembled also, and they have put it even among their own stuff.
>
> Therefore the children of Israel could not stand before their enemies, but turned their backs before their enemies, because they were accursed: neither will I be with you anymore, except ye destroy the accursed from among you.
>
> Up, sanctify the people, and say, Sanctify yourselves against tomorrow: for thus saith the Lord God of Israel, There is an accursed thing in the midst of thee, O Israel: thou canst not stand before thine enemies, until ye take away the accursed thing from among you.

Joshua rose up early in the morning and gathered the tribes of Israel.

The tribe of Judah was taken, and he took the family of the Zarhites man by man. Zabdi was taken from the group. Zabdi brought his household man by man, and Achan was taken. And Joshua said unto Achan, "My son, give, I pray thee, glory to the Lord God of Israel, and make confession unto Him; and tell me now what thou hast done; hide it not from me."

Achan answered Joshua and confessed the things he had done:

> "When I saw among the spoils a goodly Babylonish garment, and 200 shekels of silver, and a wedge of gold of fifty shekels weight, then I coveted them, and took them; and, behold, they are hid in the earth in the midst of my tent, and the silver under it."

Joshua sent messengers to the tent where all the things hid were seen. The messengers gathered the items and brought them to Joshua.

> "And Joshua, and all Israel with him, took Achan, the son of Zerah, and the silver, and the garment, and the wedge of gold, and his sons, and his daughters, and his oxen, and his asses, and his sheep, and his tent, and all that he had: and they brought them unto the valley of Achor.
>
> And Joshua said, Why hast thou troubled us? The Lord shall trouble thee this day. And all Israel stoned him with stones, and burned them with fire, after they had stoned them with stones.[1]"

---

[1] Stoning was the mode of death inflicted for certain sins in Israel, including idolatry (Lev. 20:2) and blasphemy (1 Kings 21:10; compare Acts 7:54–60).

They covered him Achan, his family, his animals; and the stolen treasure with a heap of stones.

The Lord God turned from the fierceness of his anger toward them and the name of that place was called the valley of Achor unto this day.

Bible Reference: 7:1—A Nation's Sin

This verse indicates the unity of the nation in the sight of God. The trespass was committed by Achan, one man, but his sin involved the whole nation. The principle is stated in the New Testament in the words, "No man liveth unto himself" (Romans 14:7). There is a parallel between Achan and his sin and that of Ananias and Sapphira, who lied to the Holy Ghost (Acts 5:3, compare Joshua 7:11).

Can you think of what has occurred in our country today and see some similarities? There's a saying that if you dig a ditch for someone else, you might as well dig one for yourself.

About the Author

Having been raised in a rural area of West Virginia, Constance considers herself a plain country person. Even though she is now a resident in a major city, she feels her core remains plain and country.

Her credentials include being a believer in the Lord Jesus Christ; a former school teacher; a Sunday school teacher; a missionary to seniors, the disabled, and children; a mentor for children and teens; organizer of a nonprofit mission service organization to South Africa; and a person who loves and studies the Word of God.

Constance says that the more she reads and studies God's Word, the more she feels compelled to write this book of Bible stories to be a guide for our life, particularly to be an anchor in the life of young people.